THE WEIGHT OF WORRY

Practical Approaches To Anxiety

Ethel Rojas

Copyright © 2024 (Ethel Rojas].

Table Of Content

Introduction

Anxiety is a natural response to life's challenges and uncertainties, a mechanism deeply rooted in our survival instincts.

At its core, anxiety is the mind's way of preparing us for potential threats, pushing us to anticipate danger and take preventive action.

In manageable doses, it can motivate us to meet deadlines, study for exams, or prepare for life-changing events.

However, when anxiety becomes overwhelming or persistent, it can disrupt our well-being, cloud our thoughts, and strain our relationships.

In today's fast-paced world, anxiety has become a common emotional burden.

Whether triggered by financial pressures, social expectations, health concerns, or global uncertainties, it can feel like an invisible weight, pressing down on both mind and body.

Unlike fleeting moments of worry, chronic anxiety persists, affecting how we think, feel, and behave.

It may cause physical symptoms such as racing heartbeats, restlessness, or difficulty sleeping, alongside mental distress like overthinking or fear of the unknown.

Understanding anxiety is essential to managing it.

It is not just a personal flaw or a sign of weakness but a complex interplay of biology, environment, and personal experiences.

In this book, The Weight of Worry, we will explore the roots of anxiety, how it manifests, and most importantly, how we can lighten its grip.

Through insights, strategies, and stories, this journey aims to empower readers to regain control, cultivate inner peace, and carry life's inevitable worries with greater ease.

Chapter one

Understanding Anxiety

Anxiety can be described as a natural human response to stress or perceived danger.

It is an emotion characterized by feelings of worry, fear, or unease, often accompanied by physical symptoms like a racing heart or sweaty palms.

While everyone experiences anxiety from time to time—such as before a big event or during uncertain situations—persistent or overwhelming anxiety can interfere with daily life.

In this chapter, we'll explore what anxiety is, its different forms, how it affects the mind and body.

Anxiety is a complex emotional and physiological experience that all humans encounter at some point.

It serves as a natural response to situations involving uncertainty, perceived danger, or stress.

While anxiety is often uncomfortable, it plays a critical role in helping us recognize potential threats and prepare to handle them.

In essence, anxiety is a survival mechanism, though for many people, it can spiral beyond its intended function and lead to chronic issues.

What is Anxiety?

Anxiety serves an essential evolutionary purpose:

it prepares us to face potential threats by heightening awareness and triggering a "fight-or-flight" response.

This physiological response helped early humans survive by mobilizing energy in the presence of danger.

However, in modern times, anxiety can arise even in non-threatening situations, like social interactions or work deadlines, where this intense reaction is less useful.

Normal Anxiety vs. Anxiety Disorders:

Normal Anxiety: A temporary response to a stressful event, such as a job interview or an exam.

It usually fades once the stressor is gone.

Anxiety Disorders: When anxiety becomes chronic, excessive, or out of proportion to the situation, it can be classified as a disorder.

Anxiety disorders affect approximately 1 in 5 people worldwide and require attention when they impair functioning or cause significant distress.

Types of Anxiety Disorders

Anxiety is not a one-size-fits-all experience. There are sevey types of anxiety disorders, each with distinct symptoms. It can take many forms, including:

1. Generalized Anxiety Disorder (GAD):

GAD has to do with persistent and excessive worry about everyday events.

Uncontrollable worry about a range of topics, such as work, health, or everyday matters when there is no obvious reason for concern.

People with GAD often feel restless, tense, and exhausted from constant worrying.

The anxiety is often disproportionate to the actual likelihood of impact of feared outcomes.

2. Social Anxiety Disorder:

This disorder is Characterized by intense fear of social situations where one might be judged, embarrassed or scrutinized by others in social settings.

This can make public speaking or even casual interactions feel overwhelming.

It can prevent people from attending social events or interacting comfortably with others.

3. Panic Disorder:

Panic disorder is characterized by sudden, recurrent and unexpected panic attacks—intense episodes of fear accompanied by physical symptoms like chest pain, dizziness, and shortness of breath.

People with panic disorder often worry about having another attack, which can lead to avoidance behaviors.

4. Specific Phobias:

These involve irrational fears of particular objects or situations, such as heights, spiders, or flying.

Even thinking about the feared stimulus can trigger anxiety.

The fear often triggers an immediate response of anxiety or panic.

5. Obsessive-Compulsive Disorder (OCD):

Though technically distinct from anxiety disorders, OCD involves intrusive thoughts (obsessions) that cause anxiety and compel individuals to engage in repetitive behaviors (compulsions) to reduce that anxiety.

6. Post-Traumatic Stress Disorder (PTSD):

PTSD can develop after experiencing or witnessing a traumatic event or incident.

Symptoms include flashbacks, nightmares, and heightened anxiety, in situations that reminds the individual of the trauma.

The Mind-Body Connection in Anxiety

Anxiety affects both the mind and the body, which also manifest in physical symptoms. Understanding this connection is essential for managing it.

Some common signs include:

Emotional Effects:

Restlessness, irritability, feelings of dread, or a sense of impending doom.

Cognitive Effects:

People with anxiety often experience excessive worry, racing thoughts, and difficulty concentrating.

Their thoughts may become stuck in a cycle of "what ifs," which can amplify fears and stress.

Physical Symptoms:

Common physical symptoms of anxiety include:

Rapid heartbeat
Sweating or chills
Muscle tension
Shortness of breath
Nausea or stomachaches
Fatigue

These physical symptoms occur because anxiety activates the autonomic nervous system, which prepares the body for fight or flight, even if no real threat is present

However, when this response is activated too frequently or unnecessarily, it can lead to chronic stress and emotional exhaustion.

CHAPTER TWO

Causes Of Anxiety

Anxiety is a complex emotional and physiological state characterized by feelings of fear, worry, or apprehension.

While occasional anxiety is a normal part of life, chronic or severe anxiety can interfere with a person's well-being and functionality.

Understanding the root causes of anxiety requires exploring a range of factors, including genetic predispositions, brain chemistry, life experiences, personality traits, and environmental stressors.

In this chapter, we will delve into the key contributors to anxiety, helping to uncover why it manifests differently in individuals.

There is no single cause for anxiety. Instead, it usually arises from a combination of genetic, psychological, environmental, and biological factors:

The major causes of anxiety include:

1. Biological Causes

1.1 Genetic Predisposition

Research has shows that anxiety disorders can run in families, thereby suggesting a genetic link.

Individuals with close relatives who have anxiety or other mood disorders are more likely to experience anxiety themselves.

Genetic vulnerabilities may not determine anxiety directly but can increase sensitivity to stressful life events, creating a foundation for it to develop.

1.2 Brain Chemistry Imbalance

The brain relies on neurotransmitters like serotonin, gamma-aminobutyric acid (GABA), and dopamine to regulate mood and emotions.

A deficiency or imbalance in these chemicals can impair the brain's ability to manage stress, contributing to heightened anxiety.

For instance, low serotonin levels are associated with generalized anxiety, while reduced GABA activity can prevent the brain from calming down after a perceived threat.

1.3 Overactive Amygdala and Brain Circuits

The amygdala, a brain region involved in emotional processing and threat detection, plays a significant role in anxiety.

An overactive amygdala may lead to exaggerated responses to potential threats, triggering fear even in non-threatening situations.

Additionally, poor communication between the amygdala and the prefrontal cortex—responsible for rational thinking—can impair the brain's ability to regulate anxious responses.

2. Psychological Factors

2.1 Cognitive Distortions and Negative Thought Patterns

People prone to anxiety often engage in distorted thinking, such as catastrophizing (expecting the worst outcome) or overgeneralizing (believing that one failure defines all future attempts).

These negative thought patterns fuel anxiety by making situations seem more dangerous or uncontrollable than they actually are.

2.2 Personality Traits and Temperament

Certain personality traits, such as perfectionism, high sensitivity, and the need for control, are associated with anxiety.

Individuals with an anxious temperament may feel overwhelmed by uncertainty or discomfort, making them more susceptible to chronic worry.

Introversion and behavioral inhibition—reluctance to approach new situations—also correlate with anxiety in some cases.

2.3 Learned Behaviors and Conditioning

Anxiety can result from learned behaviors, especially if someone grows up in an environment where fear is emphasized or modeled by caregivers.

For example, children who observe their parents reacting anxiously to certain situations may internalize these behaviors. Additionally, traumatic events, such as accidents or loss, can condition the brain to associate certain stimuli with danger, leading to anxiety triggers later in life.

3. Environmental and Social Factors

3.1 Early Life Experiences and Trauma

Adverse childhood experiences (ACEs), such as abuse, neglect, or family dysfunction, can significantly increase the risk of developing anxiety disorders in adulthood.

When exposed to chronic stress or trauma during formative years, the brain's stress response system becomes hypersensitive, making it harder to regulate emotions.

3.2 Chronic Stress and Environmental Pressures

Daily stressors like financial difficulties, work-related pressure, or strained relationships can accumulate over time, contributing to anxiety.

Prolonged exposure to stress without sufficient coping mechanisms can exhaust the body's ability to maintain mental equilibrium, leading to anxiety symptoms.

3.3 Cultural and Social Expectations

Cultural norms and social pressures can also be sources of anxiety.

Societies that emphasize success, productivity, or social status may push individuals to feel inadequate or fearful of failure.

Similarly, marginalized groups facing discrimination or social exclusion may experience heightened anxiety due to chronic societal stress.

4. Medical Conditions and Substance Use

4.1 Medical Conditions and Physical Health Issues

Some medical conditions, such as heart disease, thyroid disorders, and chronic pain, are linked to anxiety symptoms.

Physical health problems can create uncertainty and fear about well-being, which may escalate into anxiety disorders.

Additionally, hormonal imbalances, such as those experienced during pregnancy or menopause, can contribute to anxiety.

4.2 Medication and Substance Abuse

Some medications, including those used to treat asthma or corticosteroids, may induce anxiety as a side effect.

Additionally, substance use—particularly stimulants like caffeine or nicotine—can increase anxiety levels.

Withdrawal from substances, such as alcohol or drugs, can also trigger anxiety symptoms as the body readjusts to functioning without them.

5. Evolutionary Perspectives on Anxiety

From an evolutionary standpoint, anxiety once served as a survival mechanism.

It helped early humans detect and respond to potential threats, such as predators or environmental dangers.

In modern life, however, this system can become miscalibrated, causing individuals to feel anxious even in non-threatening situations.

The same instinct to prepare for worst-case scenarios may now manifest as chronic worry about everyday challenges.

The root causes of anxiety are diverse, ranging from biological and psychological factors to environmental and cultural influences.

For many individuals, anxiety arises from a combination of these elements rather than a single cause.

Recognizing the different contributors allows for a more comprehensive understanding of anxiety and paves the way for targeted interventions.

Whether through medication, therapy, lifestyle changes, or social support, addressing the root causes is essential for effective management and recovery.

When Does Anxiety Become a Problem?

While occasional anxiety is normal, it becomes problematic when it is chronic, severe, and interferes with one's ability to function.

 For instance, feeling nervous before a presentation is natural, but avoiding important tasks altogether due to overwhelming fear may indicate an anxiety disorder.

Chronic anxiety can impair decision-making, strain relationships, and reduce productivity.

Over time, it may also lead to physical health problems, such as high blood pressure or heart disease.

The Role of Society and Modern Life

Anxiety is not just a personal experience; it is also influenced by societal pressures.

In modern society, people are often exposed to high levels of stress, competition, and uncertainty.

The pressure to succeed, stay connected through social media, and meet others' expectations can fuel chronic anxiety.

Additionally, economic instability, global issues like climate change, and rapid technological changes contribute to a sense of unease.

Anxiety is a multifaceted experience that ranges from occasional unease to debilitating fear. It affects people in different ways, and while it can be distressing, it is also manageable with the right interventions. Understanding the nature of anxiety—how it works, what causes it, and how it can be treated—is the first step toward regaining control. In the following chapters, we will explore how anxiety develops, how it can shape our thoughts and behaviors, and the practical steps individuals can take to overcome it.

CHAPTER THREE

Effects Of Anxiety

As a natural emotional response to stress or perceived danger, anxiety in moderation can be useful, serving as a protective mechanism to alert us to potential threats.

However, chronic or excessive anxiety can have significant negative effects across multiple areas of life, including mental, physical, and social well-being.

This chapter explores both the detrimental impact of anxiety and also the positive aspects of anxiety on various aspects of a person's life.

Negative Effects Of Anxiety

1. Mental Health Consequences

Anxiety disorders are closely linked to other mental health issues, and they can significantly impair cognitive and emotional functioning.

Depression and Mood Disorders:

Long-term anxiety often coexists with depression, creating a cycle of sadness, hopelessness, and worry.

This comorbidity worsens the prognosis for both disorders, making treatment more complex.

Cognitive Impairment:

Anxiety can affect concentration, memory, and decision-making.

People with high anxiety levels often report intrusive thoughts, making it difficult to stay focused on tasks or make rational decisions.

Increased Risk of Substance Abuse:

Some individuals turn to alcohol, drugs, or medications to self-medicate, creating a dependency that further worsens their mental state.

Burnout and Emotional Exhaustion:

Chronic anxiety can lead to a constant state of hypervigilance, draining emotional resources and leaving individuals feeling overwhelmed or fatigued.

2. Physical Health Effects

Anxiety has a profound impact on physical health through the overactivation of the body's stress response.

Cardiovascular Problems:

Frequent anxiety triggers the "fight-or-flight" response, which increases heart rate and blood pressure.

Over time, this can lead to hypertension, heart disease, and an increased risk of heart attacks.

Weakened Immune System:

Prolonged anxiety suppresses immune function, making individuals more susceptible to infections and illnesses.

Digestive Issues:

Many people with anxiety experience gastrointestinal problems such as irritable bowel syndrome (IBS), stomach pain, nausea, or loss of appetite.

Sleep Disorders:

Anxiety often causes insomnia or restless sleep. Poor sleep quality, in turn, exacerbates anxiety, creating a vicious cycle.

Chronic Pain:

Studies show that anxiety can amplify the experience of pain, leading to conditions such as tension headaches, migraines, and muscle stiffness.

3. Social and Interpersonal Impact

The effects of anxiety extend beyond the individual, affecting their relationships and social interactions.

Social Isolation:

People with anxiety often avoid social situations out of fear of embarrassment or judgment.

Over time, this withdrawal can result in loneliness and reduced social support.

Relationship Strain:

Anxiety can place a burden on relationships.

Partners, family members, or friends may struggle to understand or cope with the anxious person's behaviors, leading to conflicts or emotional distance.

Reduced Work or Academic Performance:

Anxiety can impair productivity and job performance, resulting in missed deadlines, absenteeism, or poor academic outcomes.

In severe cases, individuals may even lose their jobs or drop out of school.

Fear of New Experiences:

Anxiety can prevent individuals from pursuing opportunities, such as traveling, trying new activities, or meeting new people, limiting personal growth and enjoyment of life.

4. Impact on Daily Functioning

Chronic anxiety affects an individual's ability to perform even routine tasks.

Decision Paralysis:

Anxious individuals often overthink situations, leading to indecisiveness or procrastination.

This can complicate personal and professional responsibilities.

Overreliance on Safety Behaviors:

People with anxiety may develop rituals or safety behaviors (e.g., checking things repeatedly or avoiding triggers) that give them temporary relief but reinforce their fears in the long term.

Panic Attacks:

Some individuals experience sudden, overwhelming episodes of panic, which can be frightening and interfere with daily functioning.

These attacks often result in an increased fear of future panic episodes, leading to further avoidance behaviors.

Diminished Quality of Life:

Over time, the cumulative effects of anxiety can reduce an individual's quality of life, making them feel trapped in a constant state of fear and worry.

Positive Effects Of Anxiety

Yes, anxiety can have several positive effects when experienced in moderate amounts or managed properly.

Here are some potential benefits:

1. Increased Awareness and Preparedness

Anxiety can heighten your senses, making you more alert to potential dangers or challenges.

It can lead to better preparation for important events (like exams, presentations, or interviews) because the fear of failure motivates effort.

2. Improved Problem-Solving

Anxiety signals that something requires attention, helping you prioritize and tackle problems effectively.

People experiencing mild anxiety often evaluate risks more carefully and make thoughtful decisions.

3. Boosted Performance (Eustress)

Anxiety can trigger a "fight-or-flight" response, which sharpens focus and enhances physical and mental performance in short bursts.

This is known as eustress (beneficial stress).

Athletes, performers, or public speakers often experience anxiety that pushes them to excel under pressure.

4. Empathy and Social Connection

Individuals with anxiety may be more sensitive to the emotions of others, fostering empathy and strengthening relationships.

Their heightened awareness of social dynamics can improve interpersonal skills, helping them avoid conflicts or misunderstandings.

5. Motivation for Personal Growth

Chronic anxiety often encourages people to develop coping strategies, like mindfulness or therapy, which can result in long-term emotional resilience and self-awareness.

It may push individuals to build healthier habits, such as better time management or improved self-care.

6. Survival Mechanism

From an evolutionary perspective, anxiety plays a role in keeping us safe by making us cautious of real or perceived threats. It encourages us to avoid risky situations.

While anxiety can be beneficial in moderation, it's important to recognize when it becomes overwhelming or chronic, as that can negatively affect well-being.

In those cases, seeking appropriate support is essential.

CHAPTER FOUR

Managing Anxiety – Strategies for Balance and Well-being

Anxiety as a natural emotional response to stress, uncertainty, or fear, can occur occasionally in everyday life.

However, when anxiety becomes chronic or overwhelming, it may interfere with well-being, relationships, and productivity.

Learning to manage anxiety is essential for maintaining mental health and achieving balance.

This chapter explores effective strategies for managing anxiety, ranging from lifestyle adjustments and cognitive techniques to professional interventions.

1. Self-Help Strategies for Managing Anxiety

1.1. Breathing Exercises and Relaxation Techniques

Practicing deep breathing helps to regulate the nervous system and reduce anxiety.

A common technique is diaphragmatic breathing, which involves slow, deep breaths through the nose, expanding the abdomen, and exhaling through the mouth.

1.2. Progressive Muscle Relaxation (PMR):

Tense up and release muscle groups to help alleviate physical tension.

Visualization or Guided Imagery: Use mental images to promote relaxation.

1.3. Mindfulness and Meditation

Mindfulness encourages being present and accepting thoughts and emotions without judgment.

Practicing meditation for 5-10 minutes daily can reduce the tendency to overthink or ruminate.

Body scans: Focus attention on each part of the body, noticing any sensations without judgment.

Mindful walking: Pay attention to each step, breath, and environmental sounds.

1.4. Exercise and Physical Activity

Exercise triggers the release of endorphins, which improve mood and reduce stress levels.

Activities like jogging, yoga, swimming, or even a 20-minute walk can significantly alleviate anxiety symptoms.

2. Cognitive and Behavioral Techniques

2.1. Cognitive Behavioral Therapy (CBT)

CBT has been widely recognized as a therapeutic approach for managing anxiety.

It involves identifying negative thought patterns that trigger anxiety and replacing them with more balanced, rational thoughts.

Cognitive restructuring: Identify automatic negative thoughts and challenge their validity.

Behavioral activation: Engage in meaningful activities to combat avoidance behaviors.

2.2. Journaling and Thought Records

Writing about your thoughts and emotions helps externalize worries and gain clarity. Journaling can identify triggers, track progress, and offer insights into recurring thought patterns.

3. Lifestyle Adjustments

3.1. Sleep Hygiene

Poor sleep can worsen anxiety. Adopting healthy sleep habits, such as establishing a consistent bedtime, reducing screen time, and avoiding stimulants before sleep, can improve overall mental health.

3.2. Healthy Nutrition

Diet plays a role in mood regulation. Foods rich in omega-3 fatty acids, magnesium, and B vitamins can help reduce anxiety.

Avoid excessive caffeine and sugar, which may exacerbate symptoms.

3.3. Social Support and Connection

Isolation can amplify anxiety, while social interaction can provide relief.

Stay connected with friends, family, or support groups to share your experiences and gain emotional support.

4. Seeking Professional Help

4.1. Therapy

If self-help strategies are insufficient, speaking with a mental health professional can provide additional tools. Options include:

Cognitive Behavioral Therapy (CBT)

Exposure therapy: Gradual exposure to feared situations to reduce avoidance behaviors.

Dialectical Behavior Therapy (DBT): Helpful for individuals with emotional regulation issues.

4.2. Medication

In some cases, a healthcare provider may prescribe medications such as selective serotonin reuptake inhibitors (SSRIs) or benzodiazepines.

Medications should be used in conjunction with therapy and under medical supervision.

5. Support Networks

Building a strong support network of family, friends, or support groups can provide comfort and encouragement.

Talking about fears and experiences can reduce isolation and promote healing.

Coping Strategies For Anxiety In Daily Life

1. Developing a Routine

Structured routines provide a sense of control, reducing uncertainty and promoting stability.

Include self-care activities, work, rest, and social interaction in your schedule.

2. Limiting Exposure to Stressors

Identify and manage external triggers, such as excessive work, toxic environments, or unhealthy relationships.

Practice assertiveness to set boundaries and protect your emotional well-being.

3. Acceptance and Commitment

Not all anxiety can be eliminated, and part of managing it involves acceptance.

Focus on what you can control and learn to live with some degree of uncertainty without fear.

Managing anxiety is a gradual process that requires self-awareness, patience, and consistent effort.

While some anxiety is a normal part of life, chronic or debilitating anxiety demands intervention through self-help techniques, cognitive-behavioral strategies, lifestyle changes, and, if necessary, professional support.

A combination of these methods helps individuals regain control, fostering resilience and emotional well-being in the face of life's challenges.

CONCLUSION

Anxiety is a complex but manageable condition.

Understanding its causes, recognizing symptoms, and learning effective coping strategies can empower individuals to take control of their mental well-being.

Though anxiety may feel overwhelming at times, it is important to remember that help is available.

With the right support, lifestyle changes, and therapeutic approaches, individuals can learn to reduce anxiety and live more fulfilling lives.

When to Seek Professional Help

It's important to recognize when anxiety becomes unmanageable.

If anxiety interferes with daily life, relationships, or work, it may be time to seek professional help.

Warning signs include:

Persistent worry lasting more than six months

Difficulty sleeping or concentrating

Avoiding social situations or activities

Frequent panic attacks

Mental health professionals such as therapists, psychologists, and psychiatrists can provide appropriate treatment tailored to the individual's needs.

Early intervention often leads to better outcomes.

In conclusion, anxiety is a natural emotional response to stress or perceived threats, but when persistent or overwhelming, it can significantly impact mental and physical well-being.

Understanding the different forms of anxiety—such as generalized anxiety disorder, social anxiety, and panic disorder—helps in recognizing its symptoms and seeking appropriate treatment.

Effective coping strategies include therapy, medication, lifestyle changes, and mindfulness practices, empowering individuals to manage their anxiety and improve their quality of life.

Early intervention and support from family, friends, and professionals are crucial in reducing the burden of anxiety and fostering resilience.

9 798343 101324